Words of Love

A Collection of Poems from Herman to Shirley

with other words

Rev. Dr. W. Herman White

Wake Forest, NC
www.scuppernongpress.com

Words of Love
A Collection of Poems from Herman to Shirley
with other words

By Rev. Dr. W. Herman White

©2021 The Scuppernong Press

First Printing

The Scuppernong Press
PO Box 1724
Wake Forest, NC 27588
www.scuppernongpress.com

Cover and book design by Frank B. Powell, III

All rights reserved.
Printed in the United States of America.

No part of this book may be reproduced or transmitted in any form or by any means, electronic or mechanical, including photocopying, recording, or by any information and storage and retrieval system, without written permission from the editor and/or publisher.

International Standard Book Number: ISBN 978-1-942806-40-0

Library of Congress Control Number: 2021949513

Dedication

This book of poetry is dedicated to the memory of my beautiful wife, Shirley Jean Wall White. Shirley was my high school sweetheart, whom I first saw one night at a basketball game (I think the 17th or 19th) the middle of January 1950. She was a 14 year old freshman and I was a 15 year old sophomore, and from the instant I saw her beautiful smiling face I loved her. When she was 15 and I was 16 as she was expecting a goodnight kiss, I asked her to marry me, and she immediately said that she would. Shirley was an only child and she did not want her mother to know about our plans, which would not take place until after she would graduate May 31, 1953. I had graduated May 31, 1952, and had to wait a year for her to finish. On Friday June 19, 1953, Shirley Jean Wall became 18 years of age, and June 20, 1953 we went to Dillon, South Carolina, and were married at 4 PM by Probate Judge P. Travis Ford. From that day until the angels of God came and took her to Heaven at 2:02 PM on May 21, 2019 she made our house a home.

Shirley always had a sweet smile, and her sparkling blue eyes, could light up my life, and did for 65 years, 11 months, and 14 hours. Shirley was truly an elegant Southern Belle. My Shirley Jean was truly my life, my world, and the only true love that I ever had. She was truly a gift to me from God; and Tammy Lynn McCracken insists that I was God's gift to Shirley. Be that as it may, Patricia Godwin of Selma, Alabama summed it up very well when she said, "Miss Shirley will be missed all across the South." She was indeed a faithful wife, faithful mother of Kimberly, faithful servant of our Lord Jesus, and a faithful pastor's wife, and faithful worker for the Cause of the true Southern people. I love her still, and miss her so very much, for we were always together. When I mention a certain person that loved Shirley, I usually hear the reply of "everybody loved Shirley."

— *Rev. Herman White*

Acknowledgements

Before Shirley went to heaven the lovely Kaitlyn McCracken introduced us to her mother the lovely Tammy Lynn Jones McCracken, and we became very close friends. We could feel the love from Tammy for us, as that we also had from Kaitlyn, but she left Kepley's BBQ to go to Wake Forest University to earn her Masters Degree. Therefore, we saw Tammy several times a week, and our friendship and love continued to grow. Shirley was already battling several health issues, but in early April 2019 she had a heart attack; but seemed well on the road to recovery. However, on May 21, 2019 pneumonia took her life, and the angels of God took another saint of God to her heavenly home.

Since that time Tammy Lynn has been more help to me as I continue mourning the loss of my Shirley, who was indeed my only true love. Tammy Lynn shares thoughts with me about Shirley from a woman's point of view. I told her I was adopting Kaitlyn as my granddaughter, which made her my adoptive daughter, and Dale my adoptive son-in-law; for they have been so very kind and helpful to me, and I truly love and appreciate them, (otherwise I wouldn't share my Krispy Kremes).

Thank you Tammy Lynn for helping me in my time of loss! May the Lord add to your reward in that beautiful City of God!

— Rev. Herman White

Foreword

It has been a blessing to know Rev. Herman White and his beautiful wife, Shirley. I knew the first time I met them several years ago that they had a special love story that would last forever. I was amazed that even after all the years they had been married they still had that spark in their eyes for each other, and the laughter and care they shared for each other was special beyond words. When the day came for Shirley to leave Herman's side and reap her reward in Heaven, I really began to learn how deep and special their love really was.

In this beautiful collection of poems, Herman has shared his words from his heart and the depth of his soul the declaration of the love that he possesses for his Shirley. The early years and the beginning of their lifelong romance; the desire to please and the experiences they shared. The portals they entered together and embraced the joys of their lives together. The final portal that Herman did not walk through with Shirley has not closed. His words of love and yearning are expressed in his poems of loneliness, and sadness, and the hope that he will again see his beloved bride and rejoice in eternity never to be apart again.

I am truly privileged to have been included in the celebration of their romance through Herman's works of poetry. Also included in this special tribute to Shirley are works from Shirley, Spiritual poems, and poems about people Herman has worked with over the years.

God bless you Herman,
Tammy Lynn McCracken

The Results Of Loving The Boy

Shirley at fourteen was in love with the fifteen year old boy
Even though she did not say it in words as she was being coy.
But she showed Herman that she did love him in so many ways
That she had the boy thinking about her all through the day.

So by the time that she was fifteen and he had turned sixteen years
    of age
She had him bound by those velvet chains and they entered another
    stage.
For at the end of a Saturday night date, she on the porch and he on
    the step intending to get a goodnight kiss,
Instead Herman asked her if she would marry him and the reply
    was an affirmative yes from the beautiful Miss.

A Talk With God

(I found this in one of Shirley's Bibles that was probably in the 1980s. I do not know if she wrote it or someone else. When she did occasionally write something she did not date it. I know she wrote a 3rd verse to Jim Hill's What A Day *and I have not found it yet.)*

I had a talk with God last night.
I cried oh Lord please make things right!
He said He'd all my battles fight.
I had a talk with God last night.

I prayed for Him to guide me right.
Let me find some peace and a better life.
He said He'd make everything all right.
I had a heart to heart talk with God last night.

I cried oh Lord my way gets dark,
And I need your light down in my heart.
He said I am God all by myself;
If you trust me you do not need any one else.

I said thank God for now I'm free,
Thank you for giving me the victory.
Whenever I need Him He is so good to me!
I had a heart to heart talk with God last night.
Amen!

I'm Going To Heaven

(I do not know when or where Shirley J. White found this song; but she sang it over the years as God used her dedicated life and beautiful voice to glorify Himself and to bless the thousands that heard her. I found it on four pieces of a scratch pad. May you be blessed by the message in this song. Dr. W. Herman White, Chaplain-in-Chief)

Verse 1
They tell me of a city that's far beyond the sky,
They say the population will never, never die.
And there we'll walk forever upon the streets of gold,
And in that land immortal we never shall grow old.

Chorus

Verse 2
There will be no taxes, no rent we'll have to pay,
These deeds are for your mansions we'll hear the angels say.
No washing and no mending, no clothes to look thread bare,
We'll have a snow white garment of righteousness to wear.

Chorus

Verse 3
We never shall be hungry within that happy clime,
We'll eat hidden manna, drink grape juice from the vine.
We'll meet the old time prophets in fellow ship and love,
I'm home sick now for Heaven, and to see my home above.

Chorus

Verse 4
Oh I'm going to Heaven I'm going there when I die,
I'm going to Heaven in the sweet, sweet by and by.
Angels place my order for a mansion and a crown,
And in that Book Immortal just write my full name down!

Do Not Be Late For Work
Rev. Herman White Circa 1968

The night was dark and it was late,
And Julie for a taxi cab had to wait.
She had no idea there were new rules,
To be enforced by two that surely did resemble fools.
She arrived at the locked gate as I protested
Not knowing that my effort for her was wasted.
I begged and I pleaded for them to open the gate,
But all they could say was she shouldn't have been late.

She got back home and a call from me had received,
And she thought by that gate she had been deceived.
Back down the road the taxi cab came running
And arrived at the locked gate and thought I was funning.
About the time Julie started to go back home again
Monroe had to open the gate to go, so he agreed to let her in.

Dillard explained she should not have been late,
Because all he knew was at 11:15 to lock that gate.
When I told him that they were just plain silly
Up came Monroe with an explanation that was a dilly.
He said that Melrose CEO Charles Lee Amos you must obey,
Or on your job in Melrose Hosiery Mills you will not stay.
You must not forget that it is by Charles Lee you are fed
Even if you get so outrageously mad that your face glows red.

Charles Lee, Charles Lee Monroe and Dillard did cry,
And you could tell they were afraid their job would go bye, bye.
So the next time you see either Monroe or Dillard walking around
Check their noses to see if they have become a shade of brown.

So to end this story before it is too late
Remember that all they know is to lock that gate.
Even if your life should be in danger by accident or design
Just remember all Monroe and Dillard know is that sign
That says to one and it says to all at 11:15 to lock the gate,
And if you are afraid of your job at Melrose do not be late.

Eural The Walker

Rev. Herman White
July 1969

I know a man who walks a sure enough plenty
Looking and searching for J. C. Penney.
High and low, and cold or hot,
And every time he sees her asking Dot,
Are those J. C. Penney orders ready yet?
And here she comes in a nervous fret.

Here she comes moving on the double
Knowing if they're still here she is in trouble,
Because she'll be asked by the time she gets back,
Has Herman got the J. C. Penney off the track?

So Dot, dear Dot, to check please do not wait,
Because J. C. Penney haunting you must be your fate.
So cheer up and smile as you go on your way,
Because it will all be shipped for sure today!

Two Know It Alls

Rev. Herman White July 1969

I know two guys who know it all.
If you say it is spring, they will say it is fall.
If you show them that they are wrong in black and white
They will say it makes no difference for we are right.
To admit that they are wrong they will never do,
And trying not to look bad they will begin to slur you.

Whether builder, scientist, or teacher is giving a talk,
They know more than anyone about everything even the space
    walk.
If you buy your groceries at the Big Bear
You will be told that they are much higher there.

If you say it is night, they will say that it is day.
Makes no difference about that big orange moon they will say.
Because we know about everything we are always right.
And if you say that it is day then we will say it is night.

So the best thing to do with these guys who know so very much,
Is to change their gears without pushing in the clutch!

        You are welcome Bob and Hoyt!

On Reading

October 23, 1969

If you want to know more than you know now
I will surely and gladly tell you how.
Quit reading the books of filth and trash,
Which could be easily called the devil's hash.
And turn to the Bible and read the good news
Read all about the do not's and the do's.

It will change your life immediately you will see
Because the power in the gospel will set you free.
From the penalty of sin and it's burden too,

This is what reading the gospel can do for you!

To Cursers

Rev. Herman White Feb. 23, 1970

To those of you who feel that you must curse
Just remember that to those who don't it sounds much worse.
Surely there are many other words you could say,
If nothing else, you could say is it not a beautiful day?

You may think it is big and oh so smart,
But really it gives a picture of your heart.
A heart that needs to be changed and in a hurry too,
And Jesus Christ can and wants to do that for you.

Then, instead of cursing, a song you'll have in your heart,
And when you accept Christ's salvation you'll really be smart.
From your lips there won't be cursing, but praise for Him
That saved your soul from the devil's grip, and Hell's very rim!

To My Sweet Shirley Jean

By Rev. W. Herman White
November 11, 1970

My darling sweet, sweet Shirley Jean,
You will never know how much you mean
To one who probably did not deserve
A love, so wonderful, yet I will fight to preserve.

You are still to me that teenage girl
That over 20 years ago set my heart in a whirl.
The feeling you gave me then is still the same,
Only now, of course, you carry my name.

Through the years that seem to have flown,
My love and respect for you has only grown.
I just hope that on that final day
That you will still feel the same way!

Some future day we may have to part,
But as long as I live you'll have my heart.
I thank God for your love so true,
And, honestly, without you I don't know what I would do.

You may be amused by the lines above,
But always remember you have all my love.
I may not be able to express it in words to you,
But Shirley Jean I love you, I surely do!

How To Walk In The New Year

Rev. W. Herman White
December 19, 1971

In the New Year that is about to start

I wonder if you have Christ Jesus in your heart?

If you do, then surely you know God's love

That has been given to you from above.

If you have not this love received,

Do not allow your self to be deceived,

By worldly pleasures that will steal through promises vain,

Your opportunity to escape great wrath, and pain.

Just turn to Jesus Christ with all your heart,

And for that heavenly city make a start.

There the joys of the Lord are for evermore,

And you'll always be glad He knocked on your hearts door.

So start to walk with Him today,

And be sure you don't allow anything to delay

Your journey with Him up the straight and narrow way

That will take you to the land of His endless day!

On Pleasing People

October 23, 1969

I am not nor have I been in a popularity contest,
And I couldn't please most at my very best.
Jesus could not even though He was the essence of love.
Neither will I be able to though I am born of Him from above.

As a good soldier for Him I will continue to fight,
For I know that through Him I can surely live right.
So I will strive each day his pleasure to do,
And no matter what others say, I will make it through!

No Valentine For My Shirley

Rev. W. Herman White
February 15, 1972

My darling Shirley I am glad that you are mine,
Even though I did not send you a Valentine.
You see, I was busy making the money
To make sure the comforts of my honey!

I love you, the apple of my eye,
Whose beauty is brighter than any star in the sky.
So don't worry about a Valentine of paper I exhort,
When you have me with which you can cavort!

Reflecting In God's Mirror

Rev. Herman White February 19, 1972

If you looked in God's mirror how would you reflect?
Would you see something wrong you need to correct?
Do you reflect Christ to a world headed for the pit,
Or would it be difficult to tell you from it?

Remember a robe of righteousness is all He accepts up there,
So, looking in God's mirror do you reflect a life that's bare?
Are you reflecting a life bearing the Fruit of the Spirit,
Or do you look like those who say or feel they're with it?

God is looking down from the scene you reflect from above,
And He knows what's mirrored in you life, sin or God's love.
So, why don't you quit the terms of the world's ways first,
And make things right with God and then you'll reflect Christ!

Walking With God

Rev. W. Herman White
March 1973

On top of the mountain or in the valley below
I walk with God wherever I go.
He makes a way when there seems to be none,
And I always know that through Christ the victory is won.

He walks with me each step of the way,
And He blesses my soul with His grace each day.
I'll serve my Lord until this race is won,
And there forever rest with God's lovely Son.

Victory Today

Rev. W. Herman White
March 5, 1973

When you feel there is no need to try
Remember that for you Jesus Christ was willing to die.
When you have faltered in the race
Remember there is an abundance of His grace.

To forgive your sins and your failings too,
And all He asks is simple faith from you.
Just trust in Him to make the way,
And through Him you will have victory today.

He Gave His Life
(That I Might Live)

Rev. W. Herman White
March 23, 1976

Verse 1

Jesus gave His life that I might live,

He gave to me that which only He could give.

Now His joy abounds today within my soul,

Because the Lord Jesus Christ has made me whole.

Chorus

Oh how I love Him, for He gave His life for me.

Oh how I praise Him for saving a sinner like me.

Now I long to see Him on that bright day,

So I will joyously continue in this heavenly way!

Verse 2

Now I praise His name for He died for me,

I'll gladly glorify Him for He set me free.

From the chains of sin that held me so very fast,

And gave me joy eternal, which forever will last.

Chorus

It Will Not Matter Then

Rev. W. Herman White
Circa 1976

First Verse

The things of earth will no longer matter on that morning,
When the skies are split and the saints are caught away.
Most of all I want to be among that number,
The Bride of Christ set apart in white array.

Chorus

Most of all I want to look upon the Master,
And sing praises when at last the battle is won.
To know I've won the race, hear Jesus say you've kept the faith,
And most of all I want to hear the Lord say well done.

2nd Verse

Everything down here will dim and lose its value,
When compared with all the glory we will behold.
But most of all just to look upon the Saviour
That will make it Heaven even if there were no streets of gold.

Chorus

He Saved My Soul

By Rev. W. Herman White in 1978

Verse 1

So long I walked in the paths of sin

I had no hope, nor peace within.

Then I met Christ face to face,

Started to run the Christian race,

He saved my soul, Oh, praise the Lord!

Chorus

Oh praise the Lord He saved my soul,

Oh praise the Lord well He made me whole.

Picked me up from the miry clay,

Set me on the Rock to stay,

He saved my soul, Oh, praise the Lord!

Verse 2

Now I walk with Him each and every day,

He walks with me all along the way.

All the way to heaven He'll be there,

To guide me safely with His care,

He saved my soul, Oh, praise the Lord!

Repeat chorus.

The CIA

Rev. W. Herman White
Circa 1985

Out yonder stands the CIA looking out here to see what he can see,
So he can rush up to personnel to tell it to Big Daddy.
He roams through Silver Knit on his mission true,
For he is not just maintenance, he also is Big Daddy's spy too.

So you better watch your p's and watch your q's too,
For if Albert sees something he believes is amiss he knows what to do.
He will rush post-haste up to the office of the Great White Father for sure,
And you will be charged, tried, found guilty, and hung even if you are pure.

The Fastest UPS Driver In Town

Rev. Herman White Circa 1986

There was a young man named Angel who always dressed in brown,
For Willie was indeed the fasted United Parcel driver in this town.
Up one busy street and down the other
One day he met himself coming back and thought it was his brother.

So to one and to all if you see a brown truck with flames billowing around from the front to the side.
On his route seeing his customers are getting their packages on time in one door and out the other he does glide.
Please do not worry and do not fret for those flames have not burned the brown paint off yet.
For Willie is one cool driver who even in the rain does not get wet.

William Angel the fastest UPS driver in their history!

Herman's Dixie

September 26, 2015

I felt we needed a post War of Northern Agression version of Dixie!

Verse 1

Oh, I wish they weren't in the land of cotton,
Gone back north and truly forgotten
Get away, get away, get away out of Dixie Land!
In Dixie land where I was born early on one April morn,
Get away, get away, get away from our Dixie Land!

Chorus

Well I wish they weren't in Dixie, get out, get out,
In Dixie Land I've taken my stand totally against them,
So get away, get away, get away from down in Dixie,
Get away, get away, get away from down South in Dixie.

Verse 2

They raped our women and young girls too,
Stole their food and their treasures true,
Get away, get away, get away out of Dixie Land!
They burned Dixie down and stole the rest,
So from our land we want them to travel fast,
And get away, get away, get away from off our Dixie Land!

Repeat chorus

For Shirley J. White On Mother's Day

May 12, 2002

To my beautiful wife who is the joy of my life, the young thing who left her mother, and came over to my house to live!

There is a saying that roses are red, and violets are blue,
I say there is that which is more beautiful, and that beauty is you!
    Whether it is symmetry of form, beauty of countenance, or spiritual grace,
There is no one in the whole wide world that could put you in second place.

A beautiful mother that was loving and kind to our daughter Kim,
She lived a holy life for Jesus so through her life she could see Him.
Shirley taught her the principles by which she a young lady could be,
And she always lived them before her for a show and tell to see.

A gracious, patient, and loving example of what a godly wife should be,
An example that any woman can follow, and forever in Heaven be.
This lady is my lover, friend, confidant, and wife that I love,
And without a doubt she is God's gift to me from above.

I LOVE YOU,

HERMAN

My Dear Shirley Happy Valentines Day!

(This was besides the Valentine I got for her in 2005)

You light up my life with your love and your kisses,
And I am so very blessed that you are my Misses.
You mean more to me than you could ever know,
And it still does not seem that I first saw you 55 years ago.

I love you,
Herman

To Bonnie, Our Waitress and Friend
Circa 2019

They say that beauty in motion
Are the waves of the wind tossed ocean.
But we thought it was Bonnie as she flits to and fro
Looking great in whatever direction she may go.

She may rush down to check on Double L,
But then she swiftly returns to us as well.
To make sure our coffee cup is full to the brim,
And then she hurries back down to check on him.

And when I would tell her she really looked great,
Bonnie would demur explaining she got up late.
Shirley would remind her when complimented to reply "I know,"
And I would tell her that I was an expert on her beauty's glow.

Therefore Bonnie you are to accept our compliments with grace,
Since for years we have been seeing your face.
And knowing that Shirley and Herman are experts on you,
Do graciously accept our compliments whatever you do!

You Were My World

Shirley Jean Wall White
June 19, 1935 to May 21, 2019

I would not have missed you being my wife for the world,
And I would not have missed loving you for the world.
Each day just seeing your face with that beautiful smile,
Shirley, you truly did make my life with you worth while.
Your love sent me into an awesome magical beautiful whirl,
And I would not have missed it for the world.

Married June 20, 1953

Written on our marriage anniversary June 20, 2019
Rev. Dr. W. Herman White

God blessed me to share her love as my beautiful wife for 65 years, 11 months, 14 hours, 2 minutes

Sorrowing In Hope

Rev. Dr. W. Herman White
June 26, 2019

Up there we'll be forever inside that beautiful land;
And there no evil or heart ache can ever be on hand.
There we will walk with Jesus and those that we love;
So it makes me home sick to meet them and Shirley above.

Our 2019 Trip To Mobile

(I woke up at 4:05 AM July 3, 2019 and this is what came to me.
Dr. W. Herman White.)

Shirley and I were to travel to Mobile by the bay,
But the angels of God took her away on the 21st of May.
For here on earth her work glorifying God was done,
So in Heaven Shirley's beautiful voice is praising the Son.

While back here on earth Herman's work continues still,
Awaiting His call, and continuing to do the Lord's will.
Then too the angels can fly him to see Shirley his only love,
That together then they can continue to glorify God above.

So alone I will have to travel to Mobile by the bay,
But Shirley will still be there in my thoughts all the way.
Just as the Lord said that He would never leave or forsake me,
All the rest of my time I will await seeing Jesus and Shirley.

God Gave Me Shirley

Rev. Dr. W. Herman White
September 4, 2019

My meeting her in January 1950 was not an accident,
For without a doubt to me you were heaven sent.
And it is no wonder that what might appear accidental
Was indeed a gift to me by God that was monumental!

Her touch, her laugh, her effervescent beautiful smile,
Did light up my life with her through each loving mile.
Of a loving life together that reads like a fairy tale.
Of a life so beautiful that death doesn't make it pale.

Oh yes indeed I miss Shirley's touch, her warm embrace,
But God deemed she had finished her earthly race.
So the clarion call sounded for the angels of God to bring her home through heaven's pearly gate,
And now for that glad reunion with his Shirley Herman will surely have to wait.

Until his work is done and the call from heaven is given,
Herman will keep laboring for the Lord while awaiting heaven.
For the time when again these two will be forever together again,
Where there is no sickness, death, heartache, or any thing that causes pain.

Until Then

Rev. Dr. W. Herman White
November 12, 2019

Until the rivers all have run dry,
And there are no more fish to fry,
Until Herman's life on earth is through
He will always, forever and a day, be loving you.

For Shirley Jean you were the only girl for me,
And I will be missing your touch 'til I cross that mystic sea;
And we meet again in Heaven on that glad reunion day,
And then can continue together serving God forever and a day.

Alone For Six Months

Rev. Dr. W. Herman White
November 21, 2019

I never wanted to live without my Shirley in this life,
Never really thought the day would come I'd lose my wife.
I was trusting that she would as before come home,
Not knowing that God's will was to take her to her Heavenly home.

But for 58 years, 8 months, 17 days, and 3 ½ hours we had lived
 desiring God's will be done,
Not knowing that one day one of us would be left without the one
 whose heart we had won.
And my prayer as always will still be thy will be done,
For I have the joy of knowing Shirley's victory has been won.

Yet here I am six months to the day,
Since the angels of God took my beautiful Shirley away.
I miss her beautiful smile and hearing her laughter on my ears,
And her sweet kisses that I so very much enjoyed all those years.

The pedestal I had Shirley on for better than 69 years,
Now is empty except for the puddles of my tears.
For she was the Queen of my life, my lover, and truly my every-
 thing;
She was always smiling, so surely Herman must have been her King

What My First Look At Shirley Did To Me

Rev. Dr. W. Herman White
November 22, 2019

Without a doubt I loved Shirley and she loved me,
So we went to be married in Dillon, S. C. June 20, 1953.
To me her beautiful smile and sweet demeanor were her halo,
And all across the South I and thousands of others loved her so.

For in January 1950 with that first look upon her beautiful smiling face
She captured me immediately and my heart began to race.
For this beautiful 14 year old young lady immediately bound me then and there with a velvet chain,
And she kept me enslaved with love for her until she came to me as my wife pure as a white dove is plain.

And down through the years she continued to stoke that flame;
For though Shirley might not say much she knew how to keep Herman tame.
She always said that if Herman ever left her she was going with him;
She said that she kept her little bag packed in case he got an urgent whim.

And year after year the love that filled my heart at that very first look
Not only did not diminish but the fruit of them would fill up a book.
Even as age and health issues began to take their toll I still saw that 14 year old from back in 1950;
And did try my very best to get her to understand that, to me she was still just as nifty.

So that very first look filled my heart so full of love for her there was never any room for any one else 'tis true.
And that will continue to be the way it is until Herman's life on this earth is through.
For I have the memories of Shirley Jean Wall White which will continue to fill my heart with her love,
Until God calls me to that grand reunion with her in Heaven above.

Why My Heart Is Broken

December 4, 2019
Rev. Dr. W. Herman White

I could not have loved Shirley Jean any more,
And my love for her reached from shore to shore;
And even as I was across the sea in 1973
Shirley was still the one and only love for me.

From the first look at her my heart with love was full
So there was not need for any one else to pull
And try to turn my head and heart away
For there was room for only Shirley and that's the way it will stay.

For all through the day my thoughts were only of you,
And I could hardly wait for the work day to be through,
So I could come home to see the love of my life,
And to hold in my arms, my beautiful and loving wife.

Her kisses set Herman's whole being in a magical whirl,
For this young beauty had become his whole world.
And from June 20, 1953 when Shirley became his wife
They lived, laughed, and loved with which their life was rife.

That all came to a screeching halt on May 21, 2019
For God called home the one Herman had loved since she was 14,
    and he was 15.
Before Probate Judge P. Travis Ford they had vowed faithfulness
    that only death could part,
And her death is what did and continues to break Herman's lonely
    heart.

My Friend

By Tammy Lynn McCracken
December 20, 2019

Thank you for being a friend
That will be dear to us to the end.
Thank you for your prayers
When things look bleak and dire.

Thank you for listening to us when we complain,
And help us to see when we are to blame.
Thank you for being you,
And for all that you do.

Thank you for sharing your sweet Shirley
Who was taken from us too early.
Shirley is waiting by Heaven's gate,
But she knows you will be late.

Your work is not done because you are the one that goes the extra
    mile
To make us smile.
We pray the Lord bless and keep you,
Because you are as special as your Shirley too.

Herman On Missing Shirley

Rev. Dr. W. Herman White
December 4, 2019

I miss my one true love so very, very much,
And her beautiful smile, her laugh, her loving touch.
I miss Shirley sitting beside me on our many trips,
And the sweet taste of her loving kisses on my lips.

I miss the times on our vacations across the land,
And riding for miles and miles while holding her hand.
I miss those certain looks that told of her amazing love for me,
As we traveled across this land from sea to shining sea.

I miss Shirley in her gown going through the house
And fussing because she could not find a skirt, bra, or blouse.
And when I would say a place for everything and everything in its place,
There was always a retort without that beautiful smile on her face.

I miss eating with her, especially on Saturdays, at Kepleys's Barbeque,
And the fun we had with our waitresses Kaitlyn and Tammy Lynn too.
Also sweet Shyann that got such a laugh out of our carrying on,
And that was usually interrupted by the ringing of the telephone.

I miss her sitting at the end of the pew in church which was her usual place
Always there to worship, which put a glow on her beautiful face.
Sometimes as she worshipped the Lord she would have her hands raised,
Giving glory to the Lord Jesus as she lifted her voice in praise.

I miss Shirley behind the pulpit as she worshipped the Lord in song,
And how her beautiful voice blessed so very many others for so long.
I miss the spiritual impact in our services as the Holy Ghost used Shirley,
And was such a blessing that the folks did not care if it was late or early.

Because we did so much together I miss her every where I may go,
And whether it is going to eat, on trips, or church I know
That I will miss Shirley, my dear beautiful Shirley, my only true love,
And that will be the way it will be until I go to meet her in heaven above.

Herman's Blue Christmas

December 25, 2019
Rev. Dr. W. Herman White

I will have a blue Christmas without my darling wife, Shirley;
But she is having a great time behind those gates that are pearly.
The beautiful decorations upon that green Christmas tree
Won't mean much to me, because Shirley will not be with me.

We always gave cards to each other that had messages relating to the love that we shared;
So I got a Christmas card for her titled "My Wife, My Blessing" about God's gift of love we shared.
I also decorated her tomb with a plaque stating "That Jesus is the reason for the season" so it would not be bare;
And all the while I was shedding tears for my true love for which I so deeply still care.

There are truly well meaning individuals that tell me I should not be blue;
But they really do not understand the total consuming love I have for you.

There are those that suggest that time will heal the terrible hurt and pain;
But the love that Shirley and I shared so very long just makes their wasted words vain.

Now for the first time I am observing Christmas without Shirley in 66 years;
And I am having a blue Christmas visiting her tomb and crying many tears.
But in this special time of giving and receiving gifts to honor Jesus' birth,
I will still be thankful for the gift of Shirley as my wife whose value was beyond worth.

The Prince and The Princess
(Herman and Shirley)

February 5, 2020

From the night they met at a basketball game in mid-January 1950
The young prince knew that this beautiful princess was truly nifty.
From the moment he saw this outstandingly and beautiful young lass
His heart was filled with love for her like water overflows a full glass.

This beautiful lass was only fourteen and he was only fifteen,
And as they began to date the time flew by and now they were 15 and 16.
The love of the young prince is now so great because of her sweet charm
That he decides to ask her to forever be the one to hold onto his arm.

As she stands on the porch, that night, expecting a good night kiss.
Instead, as he stood on the top step, he asked her to be my beautiful Mrs. instead of my Miss.
Immediately the beautiful young princess agreed to become my queen
Even though she was only fifteen and her prince was only sixteen.

On a Saturday date shortly after she said yes they went to Samuel Hyman Jewelry Store;
Because if he had shopped for her rings his effort might be less rather than more.
From the very beginning it was always his desire to please his princess;

And for sure the young prince in this effort wanted nothing but success.

So the prince got the princess to go with him and for her to pick the set out.
He used the lay away plan paying some each week with money from his paper route.
And when the rings were paid for she had him keep them out of view,
For her Mother did not know what her only child was planning to do.

As the young prince and princess looked to a wedding after graduation
There entered into their plans that which was a great aggravation.
For the now seventeen year old princesses' Mother discovered the plan of her only child to be married;
And she immediately set out to scuttle their plans and against them harried.

She started an all out effort to defeat what the young couple had planned.
She would have a marriage annulled and forbid the young prince to set foot at all on their land.
She then proceeded to order Shirley to date others hoping she would lose interest in the love of her life,
And in that way block the young princess from becoming the prince's wife.

But the year flew by and on April 5, 1953 a horn blew at 1304 North Main.

Herman paid no attention, but when a red light caught him at
     Commerce and Main the voice calling to him was very plain.
It was the young princess in her Dad's car, and said she needed to
     talk to me so very bad.
She said to go to Kroger's parking lot and one of her many friends
     with her would drive the car of her Dad.

As we drove up Main Shirley said you told me to tell you when I was
     ready to get married.
I will graduate May 31 and 19 days later the day will arrive for which
     I have tarried.
For I will legally become a woman then and Mother can do nothing
     to prevent me marrying you.
Therefore you can set everything up, rent us a house, and just do
     whatever you will have to do.

So the young prince rented a house at 2302 Kivett Drive with a
     furnished kitchen to be their first home.
He bought a bedroom suite and a dinette suite with legs of chrome.
Herman set up the time of 4 p m June 20 in Dillon, S. C. for their
     marrying;
And set up with Joyce Scott to make it appear they were going
     shopping.

So, in Dillon, SC, Probate Judge P. Travis Ford and Mrs. Ford as
     witness,
Performed the marriage ceremony that at 4 PM in the afternoon
     began their life of blissfulness.
The now young King and his young Queen left for Myrtle Beach,
And to them their dream of being forever together was now in
     reach.

For Valentines Day 2020

Rev. Dr. W. Herman White

On this day for the first time in 66 years I will not be able to embrace my beautiful and charming Valentine.
Nor can I give her the usual card that always expressed what she did mean to me as mine.
For the first eight months of our marriage we went to sleep in each others arms.
But about Valentines Day of 1954 I could no longer go to sleep wrapped up in her charms.

For she was now five months pregnant and had to differently lay,
But to still go to sleep with me in her arms of course Shirley came up with a different way.
There were many adjustments required along the way,
But our love for each other only grew on the way to forever and a day.

To me she was a treasure from God that was worth more than gold;
And his love for his beautiful Shirley only grew as the years did unfold.
He never dreamed the day would come when their life together would come to an end.
But on May 21, 2019 unexpectedly their Lord Jesus for her did send.

So now Herman is alone without his beautiful Shirley Jean to hold;
And the house that was once made so warm by her is now so very cold.
But as I sorrow in hope there will come a day in a future time,
When Herman will again be with his charming and beautiful Valentine.

Thank God For True Friends

Dr. W. Herman White   February 8, 2020

There are friends who could be labeled as simply fair weather;
And there are friends that always are faithful and will be forever.
It is really a joy and pleasure to find a true one too;
And it is even a greater joy and pleasure to find two.

In September 2014 Shirley and I met Kaitlyn for the very first time,
And she was so wonderfully sweet that it was no problem to write a rhyme.
From that day forward we always counted it a joy to see her smiling face,
And almost every time Shirley and I would set in the very same place.

For two years we had so much enjoyment as we laughed and loved together;
This was true even if the sun was shining or there was stormy weather.
And would you believe that two years later that this adorable young lady's mother entered into our life then?
And we quickly learned that just as Kaitlyn was beautiful, so was her mother, Tammy Lynn.

For several years we had such fun and they especially enjoyed Shirley's wit,
And they were often entertained by Shirley in sweet jest giving Herman a fit.
We had swiftly become friends with these beautiful and lovely two,
Which are of the caliber that exists in far too few.

And then the beautiful and always smiling Shirley Jean left us and went to Heaven.
For 58 years, 8 months, 17 days, and 3 ½ hours this beautiful saint of God had lived a life without leaven.
And Herman was left behind without the only true love he ever had;
But Kaitlyn and Tammy Lynn were there to lift his spirit even though they too were very sad.

And after nine months have passed and Herman still hurts so very much,
Kaitlyn is now at Wake Forest University, but Tammy Lynn is still there to give consolation for him in the clutch.
For with the wisdom that could only come from a woman's point of view
She explains what Shirley would have thought about all I for her did do.

So I thank God for friends that are indeed true
That are always there to be that emotional support for you.
And we did "live well, laugh often, love much" as the poet Bessie Anderson Stanley wrote;
And I believe that Shirley, Herman, Kaitlyn, and Tammy Lynn did that beyond a shadow of a doubt remote.

That Star Is Shirley J. White

Rev. Dr. W. Herman White
(Ode February 14, 2020 for Shirley's Valentine.)

When God created the heavens and hung the stars in their place,
In time to come one of these was named Usra Major by those that search far out in space.
Thus on God's Creation Day there was this beautiful star that was born;
And it got a new name on December 25, 2014, which was my gift to her on Christmas morn.

For now it would forever be known as the Shirley J. White Star from that Christmas Day;
And with a telescope, and its coordinates, one can see it for it is probably only a few hundred light years away.
I wonder when the angels took my Shirley Jean to be with the Lord if maybe on the way
That they might have taken her by the beautiful star named for her located in the Milky Way.

This star is located in the constellation Orion that Shirley read about in her continual reading of God's word.
For she would have read it in Job 9:9 and 38:31; and it is represented on the charts as a hunter with a sword.
The coordinates for her star are RA 11h 46m 26s D 53* 43' and it is bright.

And it will always be shining like the beautiful smile on her face, be it day or night.

The Shirley J. White must be a beautiful star as it orbits in its equatorial place;
For the one for which it is named always had a beautiful smile on her face.
And she was that very bright and shining star that always was the light of my life.
From the first time I saw her and throughout the 65 years, 11 months, and 14 hours that she was my loving wife.

Tragically memories for far too many like a flower in time will fade;
But those memories that my beautiful Star left in me shall never fade.
Even though she is gone Shirley still shines so very bright in my now very lonely life.
I loved her from the first time I saw her and throughout the blissful 65 years, 11 months, and 14 hours that she was my wife.

I miss you so very much Shirley Jean and you are still my only true love, and will always be my Star, and only true Valentine!

The End Of A Honeymoon

Rev. Dr. W. Herman White   (February 17, 2020)

Shirley and I loved all across this land from sea to shining sea;
And how memorable was that night in Phoenix, and how about the one in they spent in Boise!
It makes me think of Solomon and the love he had for his Shulamite wife,
Because my love for Shirley Jean mirrored them for she was truly my life.

Some loves live and truly and sadly some loves die,
And some will try to figure out the reason why.
Herman loved Shirley the instant her beautiful and smiling face he did see,
And she would become his very beautiful and loving bride June 20, 1953.

And as we traveled and were headed to Lincoln County, New Mexico that was famous because of Billy the Kid,
We spent the night in Santa Rosa that was a new experience for we slept on a water bed, sure we did.
It was a memorable and new experience for from the beginning we were always on our honeymoon.
And before the next morning arrived we sure felt like rockets launched to the moon.

Oh yes! I felt like I was holding Heaven in my arms that night,
But then that was truly the norm for Shirley was in my life a bright light.
And that was the reason so many said that we acted like we were still on our honeymoon;
For even into our eighties our life together was like a beautiful love tune.

For her kisses upon my lips were always so very lively and hot,
But sadly the last time I kissed her they were not.
For the death angel had come and taken my beautiful love away,
And all I have left now are the memories of them today.

Thus their honeymoon that had lasted for 65 years, 11 months, and 14 hours came to a sudden end.
For from Heaven to retrieve His beautiful child, Shirley Jean Wall White, the Lord did send.
Oh yes! Herman has the beautiful memories of those kisses that Shirley showered him with through the years;
But it keeps them fresh in my broken heart and each day floods my eyes with tears.

I love you still my sweet Shirley Jean and I always will!

What a Morning, What a Life!

Rev. Dr. W. Herman White   February 20, 2020

I woke up on the morning of June 21, 1953 wondering if it was a dream.
But for sure laying there beside me was the most beautiful lady I'd ever seen.
I do not recall if I pinched myself to make sure this scene was real;
However I do know that such a beautiful dream one cannot feel.

The beautiful young body laying warm up against mine,
Surely was most beautiful, and firm, and fine.
And when we came together the night before,
I know that this beauty was a virgin pure as the driven snow.

Is it not good to be holding each other this way!
If only it could last forever and a day.
And after we arrived at our home at 2302 Kivett Drive
The loving of Shirley and Herman continued to thrive.

Even into their twilight years you would find them still entwined in the passionate love they felt for each other.
Together these two were a model of what a marriage should be, a show and tell example for others.
He didn't spend his time off with the boys, nor she with the girls;
For it was with each other, and in each others arms, that their passionate love sent them in lovely whirls.

For they had promised before Probate Judge P. Travis Ford, and
    before God, to love each other faithfully until death;
And they proved that they meant every word and would cherish
    each other until their last breath.
What more could one say about this couple whose love was born in
    an instant in high school?
For it surely took death invading this loving relationship to cause
    her lips to cool.

But Herman and Shirley never dreamed it would end this way;
But they instead looked for their Lord Jesus to come for them each
    day.
It never entered his mind that the beautiful young bride, the
    Heaven he was holding in his arms that morning,
Would have finished her work here on earth, and that he would be
    left here still loving her and mourning.

But sooner or later his time will come to go through death's door;
And after seeing his Lord Jesus they can be together again for
    evermore.

__I still love you and miss you my Shirley Jean.__

Shirley's Rose-like Lips

April 6, 2020

This morning I woke up dreaming a poem about the loving kisses
    of my Shirley's rose-like lips.
Kisses which were so powerful that they sent waves of emotion
    sweeping over me higher than the navy's largest ships.
Those beautiful and kissable red lips did not need nor did she use
    artificial paint to color that beautiful smile;
For the Lord had blessed her with such beauty Herman would
    gladly have walked the proverbial mile.

For God blessed her very beautiful form with perfect symmetry,
And the love I had for her was surely enhanced by what I did see.
This beauty that Herman saw was certainly a serendipitous
    discovery;
And the love that immediately filled his heart was so complete there
    would never be a recovery.

And these two were so very much in love from the get go
That we had no idea just how very much that love would continue
    to grow.
We did not possess very much when we went to Dillon, S. C. to be
    married;
But we did not worry about what we didn't have for it was by our
    love that we were carried.

From year unto year our relationship was never ever bad;
For we continually gave to each other all the love that we had.
When I looked into those beautiful blue eyes I saw nothing but love forever,
For Shirley's beauty and charm to me was captivating even if she was experiencing bad weather.

We never knew how it would go or even how it would end;
But we trusted totally our Lord and Saviour, our very best Friend.
The Lord was the center of our lives that were so filled with love,
And without a doubt God's gift to each other from heaven above.

Each day we lived and loved our way on our journey to forever;
And we shared our very souls, our minds, our total selves together.
All the while expecting Jesus would soon be coming for us,
So, day by day, whatever came or went we never made a fuss.
But on May 21, 2019 Herman expected his only true love to come home from the hospital as before,
Not knowing that the angels of God were waiting just outside that emergency room door.
But they came in instead and took his Shirley to her heavenly home above;
And I kissed those rose-like lips and said goodbye to my only true love.

Watching and Seeing Shirley

April 10, 2020
Rev. Dr. W. Herman White

Down through the years I loved to watch Shirley without her
    knowing;
For to me she had such beauty and that beauty was always glowing.
If she happened to catch me and asked me why I was looking at her
    with such rife,
My answer to her was always that I simply loved to look at my
    beautiful wife.

The radiant beauty of his Shirley Jean was really something to
    behold;
And after God made her for Herman He threw away the proverbial
    mold.
Shirley's persona was so pleasant she lit up the room with her
    presence;
And when speaking of her across the South they say that to know
    Shirley was to love her in essence.

Shirley never seemed to grasp that she possessed such beauty and
    grace;
But every one that knew her always saw such a beautiful and
    smiling face. The twinkle in Shirley Jean's lovely blue eyes
To Herman was as lovely as the blue of our skies.

Down through those 65 years, 11 months, and 14 hours Shirley's beauty still intrigued me;
And this was true whether we were at home or traveling across this beautiful land of the free.
As we traveled mile after mile in my peripheral vision I would look at her lovely face;
And for mile after mile I was thinking about her love for me, which caused my heart to race.

Even in our eighties, when I looked at her, I saw in my mind that 14 year old
That sweetly called out to me in mid-January 1950, "would you get me something," and in 1953 she became mine to hold.
Herman loved watching this beautiful woman that he loved completely with all of his heart;
And now that Shirley has gone to heaven Herman misses seeing her beauty that had him so captivated from the start.

True Love Never Dies

April 18, 2020
Rev. Dr. W. Herman White

When I am asked about Shirley if I said that it hurt less now it would truly be a lie;
For I love Shirley just as much as when she left for Heaven and I know why.
From the first time I saw her beautiful face I immediately loved her and that love only grew;
And to me her love so completely enveloped and covered me it was like the morning dew.

As the poet wrote, "Loving her was easier (than anything I'll ever do again), which truly described my wife.
Shirley loved me completely, and was my joy, and my pleasure, and my world, and, in reality, my life.
Herman was totally intoxicated by her beauty, and her smile, and the love which the two of them shared.
This loving relationship kept Herman on a natural high, and also told him how very much for him she cared.

I can't explain how Shirley Jean opened every door into my mind that caused me a tingle to feel;
But I know that she loved me so totally, and so completely, that for sure the tingle never ever became a chill.

For when I looked into Shirley's blue eyes the effect was
    conjuration, and fascination, and total captivation.
And the result was such a loving relationship that it should be
    understood why without an explanation.

Since she left for Heaven everything has changed except my fervent
    love for my Shirley;
And to be without my only true love hurts each day whether I am
    up late, or if I am up early.
For through the years we loved each other totally and now Herman
    is without his beautiful Shirley;
So, what will I do without Shirley? I will keep serving the Lord 'til
    He calls, whether it be late or early.

Herman never had to chase after a rainbow for the proverbial pot of
    gold;
Because for 65 years, 11 months, and 14 hours he had Shirley to
    hold.
And since she left for Heaven even in a huge crowd thinking of her
    he cries;
For no matter how much time has passed for him their true love
    never dies.

Stepping Through Portals Together

May 21, 2020 the anniversary of Shirley's death.
Rev. Dr. W. Herman White

This poem is about some of the important highlights of our lives from the first time we met in mid-January 1950 at a Jamestown High School basketball game. Shirley was a 14 year old freshman, and I was a 15 year old sophomore; we were 4 ½ months into the school year of 1949-1950 school year and I had never seen her; not even that night as she was setting behind me. The first portal opened as I got up to go get some popcorn, and a voice called out, "would you get me something?" I turned and saw the most beautiful smile I had ever seen in my life; and I was immediately shot through the heart with Cupid's arrow for this beautiful young girl of 14.

From the very first instant I saw Shirley Jean Wall I loved her beyond measure;
And I had found a pearl of great price, and I found her love in return a great treasure.
Although Shirley was never one that did a lot of talking about how she felt;
I found that she could tell me so very much in the way she looked, or her touch that made me melt.

Essentially from the start this 14 and 15 year old pair was a steady one that never had suffered a rift;
And within a year this now 15 year old beauty and her 16 year old beau were thinking of the marriage gift.
So on this particular date night as Shirley stood on the porch expecting a goodnight kiss,
Herman instead asked her to marry him and become a Mrs instead of a Miss.

Thus these two young teens planned from that night to be married
 for her answer was an immediate, yes.
And without a doubt these two love birds walked through another
 portal in their life I will readily confess.
Even though he would have to wait a year for her to graduate in May
 1953 and to become his wife,
Herman knew that it would be worth the wait for Shirley from the
 get go had become his very life.

During that year Shirley's mother tried every way that she could to
 stop them, and came up with different tactics with a flurry;
But on April 5, 1953 Shirley saw me driving down Main in High
 Point, and at the stop light hollered "we need to talk," and
 seemed in a hurry.
As she got into the car with me she said, "I will graduate May 31,
 and I'll be 18 on June 19 and my mother cannot do a thing then
 to stop me.
So she said go ahead and set everything up that needs to be done so
 that we can marry for then I will be free.

Thus on June 20, 1953 before Probate Judge P. Travis Ford in Dillon,
 SC, Shirley and Herman became husband and wife.
And the two of us had just walked through another portal having
 pledged our love to each other for life.
That night in North Myrtle Beach, SC, we began our honeymoon,
 and for certain I know she truly was a virgin pure;
And that honeymoon lasted for 65 years, 11 months, and 14 hours
 for the passionate love they showed for each other had no cure.

Fast forward to 2:35 AM the morning of June 15, 1954 Shirley and
 Herman entered the portal of parenthood;
For after close to 11 hours of hard labor Kimberly Lynn was born,

and when I saw my love she did not look good.
My beautiful wife had suffered so very much and came very near to death to bring into this world another new life;
And one thing I could do about that was to see to it that would never again happen to my only true love, my wife.

Moving on to the morning of September 4, 1960 Shirley and Herman went through another major portal together;
For in the church service, as they were moved by Holy Ghost conviction, they walked down the aisle to the altar together truly on their way to forever.
We stood together at the altar and pledged our faithfulness in serving God in the church;
And together being faithful to our pledge we grew strong in the Lord and we never experienced a lurch.

On November 17, 1960 the Lord called Herman to preach and Shirley to be a preacher's wife.
Thus these two love birds walked through another portal of their Spirit led life.
For 58 years, 8 months, 17 days, and 3 ½ hours they happily labored together in the kingdom of God;
And through by far mostly good times, and even a few bad ones, they faithfully ever onward did trod.

When Shirley developed serious health issues, the one that had her on a pedestal gladly gave her his full attention;
And in doing this Herman did all in his power to look out for any issues and their prevention.
Yet Shirley, it seemed, was growing much more weary of fighting against it all;

And that she was actually looking for the deliverance from these issues through a heavenly call.

So on May 21, 2019 at 2:02 p m Shirley found the deliverance that she had come to desire;
For she was fighting pneumonia with a temperature as high as 103.5, which was burning her like fire.
Her Saviour and Lord had heard her prayer for the healing that she so needed;
And the Saviour sent the angels to go get her, which command they readily heeded.

For the first time since their high school days Shirley went through a portal without Herman, her true love.
This time she was carried through the portal of Heaven by the angels and into the glory of eternity above.
Shirley's work on this earth for the Lord's kingdom was now over and done;
And she is gone to be with Jesus, and to receive the crowns that she surely had won.

And on that day Herman walked for the first time since their high school days through a portal without his only true love.
And now he goes to visit Shirley's tomb and sheds tears all alone now without his love;
Today he will stand at her tomb at the exact time of her death one year after his only true love left for glory;
And as he does is looking forward to seeing his Saviour and Lord, then Shirley, and that will be the start of another story!

I LOVE YOU AND MISS YOU FOR YOU WERE NOT ONLY MY ONE TRUE LOVE AND MY WIFE, YOU WERE MY LIFE.

Words of Love

I Love You Just As Much Today

Rev. Dr. W. Herman White
June 20, 2020

Since that first look at her beautiful face, Shirley Jean was all that I
    ever really desired;
For from the very beginning my heart to her was totally wired.
I gave her totally all my love and had no more that I could give;
And that will be the case for me as long as God allows me to I live.

My Shirley Jean was like a flower that was perpetually in bloom;
And her beautiful smile, sparkling blue eyes, always lit up the room.
The brown hair that circled that always beautiful smiling face;
Was that which truly accented her beauty, gracious charm, and
    grace.

Each day of my life it was Shirley Jean in my life that was for sure
    my daily inspiration;
To get the job done with great pleasure while looking forward to
    that evening, surely stirred my imagination.
My love for Shirley Jean was fervently manifested to her in so many
    different ways for almost 66 years;
And that love is just as fervent today, but without her my breaking
    heart keeps pouring tears.

(This day would have been our 67th wedding anniversary.)

My Favorite Waitress Has A Birthday

Rev. Dr. W. Herman
June 23, 2020

There is a beautiful waitress that is celebrating number fifty-six on
    June 23;
But she sure does not look close to that age, between you and me.
She is the bestest friend that a person could ever want or meet;
And I would send her a message to that effect, but I can not tweet.

When some one tries to share a thought with her, she has to rush to
    answer the telephone;
For so very much of Kepley's business is in to go orders; and then
    you are left alone.
You try to catch her as she rushes to clean a table, and she flits here
    and then there;
From the cash register, to a table with food, she makes sure that
    your drink cup is not bare.

She is usually working at Kepley's BBQ three days each and every
    week;
And I hope you will wish her a happy birthday as to pay you trek.
I am sure that she will respond with a beautiful smile, and say;
I really do hope that you will have a blessed rest of this day!

Now I Know Lonely

Rev. Dr. W. Herman White
August 18, 2020

Wayne Herman had never ever felt lonely in all of his life;
Until the day he came home to a house without his loving wife.
Now even as he sat in a large crowd, he sat there and cried;
Because he was missing his only true love, Shirley Jean his bride.

Shirley was my life, my only love, my world, my bright sunshine;
And now she is gone and the tears flow, and my heart aches, and I pine.
I never imagined life without my love, Shirley Jean, for I was not looking for death;
For I was looking for her to come home not knowing how near was Shirley's last breath.

Now in the house that she filled with her beautiful presence making it a joyful home,
Herman comes into it now, and is continually missing her making him feel so alone.
Yes, I surely know that she awaits my arrival in God's Heaven above;
But in the meantime it still hurts for I no longer have my only true love.

Shirley Jean was truly my life and my Sunshine!

Together To Them Was A Treat

Rev. Dr. W. Herman White
August 20, 2020

For years their married life to Shirley and Herman was simply to them a total treat;
And that was true whether they were traveling across the country, or just up the street.
They might be on their way to Kepley's BBQ or to the Plaza Café where they did eat;
But wherever they were, they were two happy honeymooners, for their life together was indeed a treat.

Shirley's love was like a cool drink of water to Herman, much like an oasis to a palm tree;
And Shirley Jean could quench his thirst when she said, Herman come embrace me.
Even though that certain look, along with the invitation, started a roaring fire;
What great pleasure they received as they worked to deal with it from wire to wire.

For almost 66 years Shirley and Herman never dreamed that their treat of a life together would stop;
But on May 21, 2019 at 2:02 PM in the afternoon it did, and the reality of it hit Herman like a dirty mop.
For my always beautiful and loving Shirley Jean's life on earth did cease;
And now each day Herman feels like a pair of baggy pants without a crease.

Shirley's Beautiful Smile

Rev. Dr. W. Herman White
January 1, 2021

From my first look at this beautiful young 14 year old my love for
    her was absolutely immediate;
For on her face, under her brown hair, were two sparkling blue eyes
    and a smile that did captivate.
Those sparkling blue eyes above that captivating smile turned my
    world completely upside down;
And from that night my heart always began to beat faster whenever
    Shirley was around.

With my beautiful smiling Shirley as my wife it was always you and
    me;
And she turned me every which way but loose as we loved from sea
    to shining sea.
Her beautiful smile, and special touch, brought a lifetime of
    honeymoon memories wherever we traveled for sure;
From that first night of our marriage in Myrtle Beach, South
    Carolina until Shirley left for Heaven those memories were
    without any demur.

Woodland, Washington was the nearest place for a motel when
    we went to visit the area after the eruption of Mt. St. Helens,
    volcano;

And as we experienced the wonder that the eruption caused Shirley
   still had that smile, wouldn't you know?
I had her willing to fly up into the crater in a helicopter when
   clouds moved in, and then the pilot wouldn't fly;
And Shirley smiled as she explained that the Lord did that to save
   her from having to fly was the reason why.

The memories of her smile during our stay at the Howard Johnson
   Motel at the Rainbow Bridge;
And how she was unbelievably still smiling after the helicopter
   flight over Niagara Falls had arrived back on the ridge.
How about the time along the Oregon Trail, and the smile when I
   suggested we walk around Independence Rock;
She very sweetly declined, as she was saving her strength for a
   honeymoon rock around the clock.

Whether Shirley and Herman were in South Dakota at Wild Bill's
   grave in Deadwood, or at Mt. Rushmore;
Or at the Little Big Horn Park, or the beautiful Yellowstone
   National Park, the smiles were truly galore.
My Shirley Jean, no matter the time of day or night that we
   returned back to our home was truly all smiles;
For now we had arrived back home and could sleep in our own bed
   after traveling many thousands of miles.

A Beautiful Student

January 7, 2021   Rev. Dr. W. Herman White

Shirley and Herman met this young woman in September 2014 for the very first time;
And she was so very sweet that it was no problem for me to write a rhyme.
It was always a joy to see her smiling face;
And most of the time we sat in the same place.

If we arrived, and instead of a smile there was a frown;
Then it was because of what that mean cook was putting down.
I think there were those who were jealous of this beautiful young woman that was so very smart;
And instead of being happy to work with some one so pleasant, that cook's attitude toward her was outrageously tart.

But Kaitlyn Lauren put up with such treatment without striking back;
Because she was so smart she recognized that person really did lack.
However this beautiful young woman, with God's help, did continue through it all;
And she only left Kepley's BBQ when she had to leave as she was entering Wake Forest in the fall.

Shirley went to Heaven after this beautiful young hung on to her
    desire to hit the books;
And as days turned into weeks, and weeks into months, she also
    weathered the academic kooks.
And in the fall of 2020 she received the desire of her heart, the
    much coveted Masters Degree;
And she was so thrilled to have her thesis accepted, for she had
    such concern about it she now felt free.

This beautiful, loving, and intelligent young lady made such an
    impression upon me, as she "oughter;"
Therefore, I have named her my beautiful, very smart, and truly
    loved "adoptive" granddaughter.
Her adoptive grandfather prays daily for this special lady that he
    lovingly calls the Student;
For he desires the best for her in the future relative to an academic
    position whether it comes by design or accident.

He also prays that some young man that will love her with all of his
    heart will come into her life;
For I do truly believe that she would be as wonderful a spouse to
    him, as is her father's wife!

Thank you Dale and Tammy Lynn for Kaitlyn Lauren! I love y'all!

Were We Too Young?

Rev. Dr. W. Herman White
January 30, 2021

From the first time that Herman saw her smiling face he loved that beautiful young girl;
For her sparkling blue eyes, and the brown hair surrounding her lovely face truly set his heart in a whirl.
He loved Shirley from the instant that he saw her on that middle of January 1950 night 'tis true;
And though she never told him the same was true for her, yet from that night they immediately became a steady two.

Shirley was 14, and Herman was 15, and he immediately knew that he wanted her for ever and a day to be his wife;
And, as a result, when she was 15 and he 16, he popped the question truly desiring to be her love for the rest of his life.
It was going on two years before her Mother learned that they planned to be married after they finished school;
But Mother thought she was too young, and that Shirley needed to enjoy life before marrying any one was her rule.

Was Herman and Shirley really too young to fall in love?
I believe we know the answer as well as God above!
For, before she went to Heaven, the 65 years, 11 months, and 14 hours of wedded bliss;
Proves beyond any doubt that we were not too young, and Herman still misses her kiss.

My beautiful Shirley Jean I still love you and miss you so very much; and I will until the day I die; and you are still my only Valentine!

I Loved To See Her Smile

Rev. Dr. W. Herman White   February 14, 2021

From that January night in 1950, when I first saw her, Shirley had a beautiful smile on her face;
And from that night I not only loved her, but I did all I could to keep that beautiful smile in place.
To do that required that I not only worked a first shift job, but also some of the time an evening shift;
For if there was something that she wanted then I got it for her, for I wanted to give her sweet spirit a lift.

For example, we were in the highest priced ladies store in town as she was just looking and wishing,
When she saw a Mouton fur coat that I could tell, as she felt it, had her more than wishing.
Therefore, I suggested that she try it on, and when she did you should have seen that beautiful smile;
And Herman knew that to buy, and pay for it, for her he would gladly walk that extra mile.

She protested that it was way too much for me to pay,
Knowing that Herman would get it for her if there was a way.
Herman got the sales lady to set up a charge account, which he would pay;
And I have a picture with her smiling in her Mouton fur coat that I cherish even today.

I miss seeing her beautiful smile since the Lord took her to her heavenly home, as she had finished her earthly race;
But I have no doubt as to whether or not she still has a beautiful smile on her beautiful face.
My beautiful Shirley Jean our Lord knows that you are still, and always will be, my only Valentine;
And if you could see the big Valentine on your tomb, then you would know you will always be mine!

I Don't Want To Get Over Shirley

Rev. Dr. W. Herman White
March 2, 2021

I could not get over Shirley Jean and missing her sweet love if I tried.
If you should ever hear that I have it will be because Herman died.
It has been 71 years since the first time that I saw her beautiful face;
And loved her at once with an all consuming love that made my heart race.

So, how could I erase all of the memories of sharing such an awesome love?
How could Herman ever forget her laugh, her touch, even though she is now in Heaven above?
From the time that Shirley bound me with those velvet chains of her love that was so very sweet,
I was consumed with a desire to please her, which pleased me from my head to my feet.

How could I forget the things that we said to each other no matter the weather?
Can any one tell me how to forget the many things that we did, and shared, together?
How in this world could I ever un-love my beautiful Shirley that was my loving wife;
For all of those 71 years, of which 65 years, 11 months, and 14 hours she was my wife, and my life?

Therefore, I could not, nor do I want to get over all that we shared together, which I do miss.
For after 71 years of memories, especially those that we experienced during 65 years, 11 months, and 14 hours of wedded bliss,
Herman does not want to get over his beautiful Shirley;
And he only will at his death whether it be late or early.

Their First Kiss

Rev. Dr. W. Herman White
March 14, 2021

Shortly after I met the beautiful Shirley Wall in January of 1950,
We started to date on Saturday nights, which to me was nifty.
I was fearful of doing something that would cause me to lose her
    that I had loved from the start;
Therefore, even after dating for about 2 months worth of Saturdays
    I had not even tried to kiss her, which tortured my heart.

One Saturday my married sister, Irene, asked us to go to see a Roy
    Rogers movie at the Tar Heel Drive-in;
And I decided that I was going to kiss her during the movie, and
    trust that I would end up with a win.
Shirley would have Migraine headaches come on at times, which I
    did not know, and she didn't tell.
So, I embraced her and kissed her beautiful rosy red lips, and
    Shirley did respond very well!

Shortly thereafter, Shirley said that she felt sick and had to throw
    up;
And, of course, I scrambled to find her a very much needed cup.
From that night, until my beautiful Shirley went to Heaven, she
    enjoyed telling that my first kiss had made her sick;
But Herman loved the fact that down through the years Shirley was
    truly a dynamite kisser that was more powerful than 1 dynamite
    stick.

Shirley and Herman Stood Side By Side

Rev. Dr. W. Herman White
March 20, 2021

The beautiful Shirley Jean was truly from the get go my very life;
And from the night I met her I desired that she would be my wife.
Then on June 20, 1953 in Dillon, SC, my desire became a reality;
And the two honeymooners then began a long life of marriage that exemplified fealty.

When we were married, we promised faithfulness before God and man;
And we stood side by side totally in keeping with the plan.
The plan was to love each other 'til death the two of us did part;
So, our great love and affection, each for the other, came from our heart.

Side by side we were the anchor in the storm for each other that held us firm.
Side by side we were the sunshine that a life of loving pleasure gave us in each turn.
We were side by side when decisions were to be made whether big or small;
For the two of us lived to please the other, and in love were at each others beck and call.

Down through the 65 years, 11 months, and 14 hours that God
    gifted us to share our life together,
We stood together side by side as we traveled the road of life
    regardless of the nature of the weather.
In the twilight time of our honeymoon life together, and Shirley
    had developed some health issues, I gladly stood by her side;
For this beautiful holiness lady's example of what a godly pastor's
    wife should be, surely had stood by this preacher's side.

Side by side the two of us shared a life of effervescing joy and
    pleasure;
And that life together was one that truly indeed was a God given
    treasure.
Shirley truly fought a good fight, had finished her course, and the
    angels of God took her to her Heavenly home;
And now I get so lonely, because she no longer is by my side, and
    the death of my wife has left me so all alone.

I Was Shirley's Choice

Rev. Dr. W. Herman White
March 17, 2021

It is truly amazing that out of all the young boys in all the world
That Shirley Jean Wall picked a poor farm boy to truly be his girl.
To me Shirley was amazing, and totally produced a work of fascination;
And my feelings for her were totally love, not just a brief infatuation.

When I met her, all the money I had came each week from my paper route.
So it was not worldly goods that I used to win Shirley that I did tout.
It was simply that I placed her on the pedestal of my heart:
And we always lived to please each other from the very start.

Shirley was what made the sun shine brighter every day of my life;
For this beautiful lady was a gift from God that became my loving wife.
There were other young men that were green with envy, because she had chosen me, so I have been told;
But on this St. Patrick's Day I want you to know that in January 1950 at the end of the rainbow I found a treasure more precious than gold.

My Hope On This Good Friday

Rev. Dr. W. Herman White
April 2, 2021

We stood together when reciting our vows with no way to know
The future in a world where every thing changes, and does come and go;
Herman and Shirley had no way of knowing if they would have the other to always be there to hold;
But forever came to a screeching halt at the moment Shirley left for Heaven,
And his last kiss was upon her lips death had made cold.

We had always desired, and felt, that we would leave this world together;
And be with our Lord and Saviour in the beautiful place called Heaven forever.
There were times that we talked about how things were changing so rapidly from day to day;
But we never dreamed that there would come a day when we would have to part: no, absolutely no way.

However, we do not know the future, but Shirley and Herman truly knew the One that is the Way;
And he, although he knows that she waits for him Heaven, now truly hurts so very much on this Good Friday.
Yet I am thankful to God that my Lord and Saviour knows how much I miss my only true love, and the awful pain;
And Herman knows that because Jesus came out of that tomb victorious on resurrection morn, and that he will see his Shirley again!

He is not here: for he is risen, as he said. Come, see the place where the Lord lay.
(Matthew 28:6)

A Taste Of Love

Rev. Dr. W. Herman White
May 19, 2021

My first taste of Shirley still lingers in my heart and on my mind;
For the love that we as young teenagers shared was truly one of a kind.
Our age made no difference though we were surely very young;
For even into our eighties the taste of it continued in our hearts, and on our tongues

My beautiful Shirley had blue eyes, brown hair, and the most beautiful smile in the world;
And the taste of her awesome kisses down through the years always sent Herman in a whirl.
The taste of love that Shirley and Herman shared from the very start,
Truly continued until the last beat of the beautiful Shirley Jean's heart!

There Is 100 % Chance of Pain Today

Rev. Dr. W. Herman White
May 21, 2021 2:02 PM

On June 20, 1953 at 4 p m, in Dillon, SC, the beautiful Shirley Jean Wall became Herman's wife;
And thus began what Tammy Lynn McCracken declares surely was a unique married life.
Shirley was Herman's teenage Queen, and he was her teenage King;
And their love for each other was as fresh as flowers blooming in the Spring.

These two lovebirds were completely devoted to each other from the start;
And these young lovers kept their relationship fresh as love filled their hearts.
Seven years into their marriage they went to the altar together, and their relationship with God then enhanced everything;
For now they learned that the blessings of God could even cause their love for each other to grow, because of what the Lord's presence did bring.

We had so much pleasure in love as we traveled down life's highway to forever;
And it always kept our love so very much alive as we were having so much fun in that endeavor.
We enjoyed a relationship of love that surely must have been as deep as the deepest ocean;
And we believed it to be strong enough that it could climb Mt. Everest; yes, that was our notion.

For 65 years, 11 months, and 14 hours these two were more in love than when it started way back then;
And Herman had no idea that his beautiful Shirley Jean would never be coming back home again!
This brings us to the present, like that of a weather forecast of a certain percent chance of rain;
And the forecast for me on this 2nd anniversary of her leaving for Heaven is that Herman has a 100 % chance of pain.

I know there will be pain, for I have been hurting every hour of every day;
And it will keep hurting until the angels of God come and take me away.

A Beautiful Shining Star

Rev. Dr. W. Herman White
June 2, 2021

There are many heavenly bodies in the heavens that are so very far above;
And one of them is the Shirley J. White star I had named for my only love.
Shirley was indeed the very beautiful shining star in my life;
And without a doubt this beautiful star God surely gave me to be my wife.

Her sweet demeanor emanated from within a heavenly body that was symmetrically perfect;
And I, since I was the only one privileged to inspect it in totality, was unable to find one defect.
Herman was never able to get Shirley to understand that truly she was a beautiful star;
But he kept trying down through the years however he was never able to get that far.

Another poet wrote that "She don't know she is beautiful though time and time I've told her so."
I could say the same about the shining star that did light up my life as only I do really know.
There can be no doubt that this beauty caused others to stop and stare;
And , no, it never bothered me for there was nothing but trust between this pair.

The beautiful Shirley Jean for 65 years, 11 months, and 14 hours was truly my Morning and Evening Star;
And it did not matter where we were she was always the most beautiful one by far.
May 21, 2019 the angels of God came to take her to her Heavenly home at 2:02 in the afternoon that day;
And now I am left all alone without her awesome love to shine its light upon me every day!

June 15, 1954 2:35 AM

Rev. Herman White

A momentous day for Herman and Shirley happened again;
But probably more for her as she suffered the terrible pain;
For this young mother came so very near to death's door;
And Herman would see to it that she wouldn't suffer like that any more.

The result of her suffering so much was that early that morning a new baby came into the world;
And this beautiful blonde baby name Kimberly Lynn did set Herman and Shirley's hearts in a whirl.
Kimberly had a beautiful smile just as did her mother Shirley;
And by 8 months she was talking, and some thought that was early.

Time seemed to swiftly pass and as she grew so did her love for the dogs and cats.
And Shirley said that in school work she was just like Herman in her grade stats.
Time swiftly passed as this beautiful blonde girl grew into her teenage years;
And it seemed such a short time since the first day in daycare brought tears.

In June 1972 she graduated from Ragsdale High School, and on the 15th of June was her 18th birthday;
And entered GTCC, and it would seem so quickly that our Kimberly would then be going her own way.
There was now an empty place in the room that had been her private place;
For now she was married and had for sure entered the real world race!

June 19, 1935

June 19, 2021
Rev. Dr. W. Herman White

June 19, 1935 started out with a very beautiful morn;
For later that day a beautiful blue eyed star was born.
This beautiful baby's given name was Shirley Jean;
And from an infant she had the most beautiful smile to be seen.

As she grew into the young teen years she was beautiful beyond measure;
And without a doubt she would become some young man's shining treasure.
Shirley met that young man in January 1950 when she at age 14 was at a basketball game;
And from that night forward 15 year old Herman would never indeed, could never indeed, be the same.

For he loved her from the instant that he saw that beautiful smile;
And she was the light of his life as they traveled the road of love mile after mile.
Their love was young, but it was truly a fervent love;
And it would continue to be until Shirley went to Heaven above.

Every day that they had together to Shirley and Herman was to them a blessed day;
And, since Shirley has been called to Heaven, Herman has looked forward to that blessed day;
When his work will be done, and the call from his Lord will take place;
And another blessed day will take place when he again will see Shirley's beautiful smiling face.

Happy birthday Shirley, and you are still the only love I ever had!

Thank You For Loving Me

June 20, 2021
Rev. Dr. W. Herman White

On this date in Dillon, SC, you became my beautiful wife;
And until May 21, 2019 when you went to Heaven you were my life.
You had me wrapped around your finger from the very start;
And I am still wrapped around it as you always will have my heart.
Thank you Shirley for loving me!

Day by day I go to visit your tomb as I always am thinking of my sweetheart;
And I admit that I never entertained a thought that you and I would ever part.
I reminisce about how blessed I was that you surrounded me with your constant love;
And how that you indeed was truly a gift from God to me from above.
Thank you Shirley for loving me!

Your wonderful love kept me on a perpetual Shirley induced high;
For your beautiful smile and that certain look always drew me nigh.
Someone once wrote that "in every life surely someone comes along;"
And without a doubt your love indeed made our life like a song!
Thank you Shirley for loving me!

A beauty like yourself surely had many that would loved to have had you in their life;
But you rejected them all, and out of those many you chose to be Herman's beautiful wife.
Meanwhile you have gone to Heaven and left me with all those beautiful memories of holding you;
But I will never get to hold you again as you loved for me to do!
Thank you Shirley Jean Wall White for loving me!

First Love Can Only Happen Once

Rev. Dr. W. Herman White
October 2, 2021

Just as the rivers flow down from the mountains, across the plains, and on down to the sea;
So was the first, the forever, and true love that Shirley and Herman shared was truly meant to be.
Herman's love for Shirley was so very great that she made even the star's twinkle brighter for sure;
And that love caused the light from the moon and the sun to dim in light of this love so pure.

There are those that search for, and dream about, such a love filled life;
But Shirley and Herman found it as teenagers when at age 18 and 19 they became man and wife;
And what a wonderful love affair that these two love birds enjoyed on the way to forever;
And it can be said without a doubt that Shirley had him wrapped around her finger, as she was very clever.

From the very start Herman was amazed at this beautiful and always smiling gift from God;
And since the Lord had placed her love so deep into his heart he was very careful how he trod;

For he would love and cherish Shirley who was always such a
  smiling beauty;
Because his deep love for her was so great, and it did not arise out
  of a sense of duty.

The love that Shirley and Herman shared cannot happen in peoples
  lives twice;
Therefore they were always working to keep their honeymoon
  fresh, which made it so nice.
Then on May 21, 2019 the angels of God came to take Shirley to her
  Heavenly home;
And Herman is left with a broken heart, for what they had enjoyed
  together he cannot have alone!

The Heavenly Company

(A program for young people's service written and given by Shirley J. White circa 1965)

Good evening Ladies and Gentlemen:

Tonight I would like to tell you about the most wonderful product in the world. This product is unconditionally guaranteed by our sponsor, The Heavenly Company, to work every time it is tried. The name of our product is "SALVATION," and once you have tried it you will never want to be without it.

In the world in which we are living in we find all kinds of advertising claims being made for the hair, eyes, skin, and yes even for our feet. But this world is not concerned with the most important part of our being; and that part, ladies and gentlemen, is the soul. This old body someday will go back to the dust of the earth from which it came; but our soul will live on forever. As the word of God says in Matthew 16:24 to 27: "Then said Jesus unto his disciples, If any man will come after me, let him deny himself, and take up his cross and follow me. For whosoever will save his life shall lose it: and whosoever will lose his life for my sake shall find it. For what is a man profited, if he shall gain the whole world, and lose his own soul? Or what shall a man give in exchange for his soul? For the Son of man shall come in the glory of his Father with his angels; and then he shall reward every man according to his works." That is the reason why tonight I want to tell you something about our product.

I'm sure that you have heard how Comet cleans and how it goes down and gets stubborn stains; but after you have used it for a while the container becomes empty and useless; and then you have to buy more. Now my friends just take SALVATION and apply it to the most sin stained heart and it will become as white as snow. This product will never run out, and the best part about it is that it is free; and it is for every one if they will accept it. For in Romans 6:22 we read these words: "But now being made free from sin, and become servants to God, ye have your fruit unto holiness, and the end everlasting life.

I am sure too that you have heard how ADORN helps you control your hair, but it is only for your hair. However, the product I offer you for the hair, but for controlling your temper, your tongue, helps your feet to walk in the straight and narrow "which leadeth unto life," as a matter of fact ones whole being.

On television, newspapers, magazines, and signs along the highways we continually have seen and heard their claims of how to be completely refreshed. But the world does not know what being really refreshed means. However, The Heavenly Company's product guarantees the results of their product. For to be really and truly refreshed apply our product, which is SALVATION, to the heart; and then attend meetings with others that have accepted our product. For one can then listen to the words of our Sponsor, and it surely is refreshing. Oh no! This refreshment does not come in a bottle, but from the Lord Jesus Christ. And to your delight you do not have to pay a deposit if you take it with you as you begin your journey with Jesus, for He has already paid it.

Words of Love

(XXX)

Another advertisement you will often see is "Adult Entertainment," and no one under 18 is allowed to partake of the product they are offering. However I am so glad that the product that I am telling you about tonight is not only for adults, but SALVATION is for the young as well.

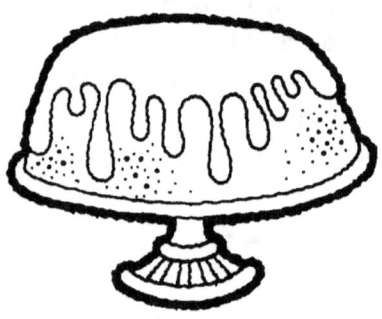

As you know we have all kinds of recipes for pies, cakes, desserts, and about anything you can think up. But try as one might so much of the time the recipes will fail. But tonight I would like to give you a recipe that never fails. It is as follows:
Take one sinner
One old time altar
Add the convicting power of the Holy Ghost
Mix well in a small, medium, or large church
And the result will be SALVATION
Oh yes, it will work every time, and the result will be another soul saved from sin and hot flames of Hell.

So, my friends, if you do not as yet have this product in your home, yes, even in your own personal life, my advice to you is this: "STOP, LOOK, AND LISTEN to your heart tonight. Please "YIELD THE RIGHT OF WAY" to our Sponsor and take this product home with you. It will be the best investment you will ever make. Remember the product's name is SALVATION and it is free. And our sponsor THE HEAVENLY COMPANY DOES unconditionally does guarantee this product. And as King David wrote in Psalm

35:9, "And my soul shall be joyful in the Lord: it shall rejoice in his salvation." And as the Holy Ghost moved Peter to write in I Peter 1:8 & 9, "Whom having not seen ye love; in whom, though ye see him not, yet believing, ye rejoice with joy unspeakable and full of glory: Receiving the end of your faith, even the salvation of your souls."

In closing my program tonight I would like for you to hear from some very satisfied customers.

And then Shirley gave the folks an opportunity to testify about THE HEAVENLY COMPANY'S GREAT PRODUCT called

SALVATION ! ! !

A Southern Gentleman, Carlyle Herring

Rev. Dr. W. Herman White
October 12, 2020

Carlyle Herring was indeed a Southern gentleman, compatriot, and friend;
He not only loved the Lord, but he loved the beautiful Judy to the very end.
I loved to kid him about the time he didn't go to the S. D. Lee Institute with his beautiful Judy;
But he would grin and say Dallas, Texas was just too far, and thus for them to stay at home was his duty.

But we all know Carlyle indeed did love his beautiful wife;
And serving the Lord together was an important part of their life.
Being a true friend was always extremely important to him;
And his friends knew for sure that he indeed truly cared for them.

So as we commemorate a life that was well lived before man, and before God;
We know that Carlyle left a record that others could follow as the path of life they trod.
Yes, Carlyle will be missed by all that knew him as a friend;
But let us please take heart for this is truly not the end.

For Carlyle kept the faith, finished his course, and now he is enjoying the glories of Heaven above this day;
And all those that will faithfully serve the Lord Jesus Christ shall surely join him in Heaven one day.

To Unhappy Employees

Rev. W. Herman White
November 4, 1969

To those who gripe about Melrose being such a bad place to work
Should stop and consider that if it's true then you are a jerk.
For why would one continue to stay in a place that is so bad,
When they could go somewhere else and make the happy ones glad.

When the boss is gone with threats they lift their voices up,
But when he comes back they are as humble as a little pep.
Because they themselves have never made any accomplishment,
All they can do is cause those around them torment.

If there are so many other fine places to which you could go
Why do you not try them out and make all that dough?
If you indeed think that to change jobs you would gain,
Please do and help the other Melrose employees get rid of a great pain.

From A Happy Melrose Employee

Judgment Day

Rev. Herman White

Judgment day is coming this I surely know:
When all the great and small shall line up row upon row.
They will cry and beg for merry, but mercy now has ceased;
Because they turned away His love and lived just as they pleased.

Then they will hear the tragic words depart from me forever more;
For you have rejected all my mercy and love, and now there is no more.
Therefore now the time has come when you are rejected to;
And this is the very final result of what you decided to do!

Epilogue

What a legacy! Herman and Shirley's life story and love story is an inspiration to other couples who are on their own journeys through this earthly life. They were the perfect example of a Christian couple. We don't remember when we first met Herman and Shirley, but it seems like we knew them forever.

All across the South at many different events, we would see them and Shirley always greeted us with that infectious smile for which she was famous. Shirley was always smiling when we saw her and Herman was never far from her side. They were special people and we're glad to help Herman publish his poems, which really are a story of a great couple, their love and their journey through life.

— Frank and Sara Powell

www.ingramcontent.com/pod-product-compliance
Lightning Source LLC
Chambersburg PA
CBHW052116110526
44592CB00013B/1638